Software Testing Series

Vol 1 – Basics
(Revision 2)

Written by:
Michael Pasono

Contents

Overview

About the Author

Michael Pasono, CISSP is the author behind the _Software Testing Series_ who systematically lays out the different areas and concepts of software testing to assure the right level of software quality. Technology is continuing to evolve at a rapid pace, this series is meant to familiarize yourself with key software testing concepts.

Michael's professional experience and advocacy in systems quality improvement has him recognized as an industry leader in technology innovations and assuring high quality systems leveraging real-world experiences.

Michael shares key quality topics and recommends approaches to ensure a high-quality product is being produced. The recommendations are provided by Michael and not any paid sponsors or previous employers.

Why Important

This Software Testing Series was written to help educate new and advancing software testers that specialize in assuring the quality of a software product or service.

As technology advances rapidly, more software quality control methods are needed to assure proper software quality. These books are meant to introduce you to key topics for you to explore and see how they might fit into your role as a software tester or software quality manager.

The Software Testing Series will be shorter books but focused on a particular topic that might be more relevant to you in your current career. They will range from basic introduction to advanced topics.

We realize time is precious for us in the software testing business trying to keep up with not only new technology but ways to assure quality being produced. This series was meant to be quick reads getting to main topic points and recommendations.

Companies

Large companies are modernizing their technology at a rapid pace to keep up with consumer expectations of an always-on product or service. Companies are taking on new challenges such as digital transformations and cloud migrations.

Not only are these large-scale changes occurring, but on-going new threats are also appearing more rapidly. These threats are around cybersecurity and data privacy. Board members, shareholders, and CEO's need to address to reduce risk.

With companies collecting so much data as it provides more value, they must hire quality experts to keep this technology humming and data safe to assure their brand reputation and stay in business. Those of you in the quality assurance and control areas need to stay current or even ahead of these changes coming.

Quality Management Umbrella

Quality management practices have been around for decades. This concept is having a systematic approach to assure processes and control quality testing has transitioned from manufacturing into engineering. This series will cover topics from both Quality Assurance and Quality Control best practice.

Here is a quick overview of the difference. This is a key area to understand before moving into the series.

Quality Assurance is all about setting up the process in which to conduct quality control. Think of it as umbrella over most testing activities execution. This explanation has helped guide the path to really identifying where in the development life cycle this quality topic falls into.

Quality Control is mainly about the execution of processes defined in Quality Assurance. Testing heavily falls under the control section.

Many companies interchange Quality Assurance with Testing only activity. This is false pretense, and this series should debunk that notion of equality.

Software Development

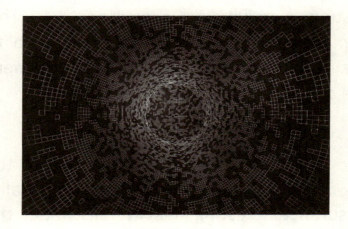

Obviously, software testing has a great deal of interaction with how software should be developed and tested. Software development has rapidly evolved over the years, making changes to existing quality control methods and creating new methods.

This series goes over many areas of the software development lifecycle such as requirements to implementation into production and applies key quality assurance and control best practices.

The Software Testing Series

The goal of this series is to introduce new and advanced topics to those interested in learning how to adopt best practices in Quality Assurance and Control.

Key series topics will include the following from those of you beginning your career in software testing to more advanced to help boost your career to that next level:

1) Basics
2) Test Strategy
3) Functional Testing
4) Performance Testing
5) Security Testing
6) Automated Testing
7) Test Data Protection
8) Advanced Methods

Chapter 1 – Basics: What is Software Testing

Definitions

What the heck is software testing? If you are new to software testing many of these key terms are new to you. Within this series we will bold new key terms that are relevant to software testing and provide the definition at that point in time.

Many official testing related definitions are provided by ISTQB and other reputable sources. We will take these standard definitions and expand on key areas throughout this series.

Software is the entire set of programs, procedures, and related documentation associated with a mechanical or electronic system and especially a computer system.

Testing is the process consisting of all lifecycle activities, both static and dynamic, concerned with planning, preparation and evaluation of a component or system and related work products to determine that they satisfy specified requirements, to demonstrate that they are fit for purpose and to detect defects.

Software Testing is defined as an activity within Quality Control to check whether the actual results match the expected results and to ensure that the software system is defective or bug free.

Testing Levels

Testing levels are a systematic approach to different types of software testing and who should conduct those activities have formed. Below is a breakout of these, focused on testing level areas along with the reasons why they are so important to validate a quality product or service is being produced.

Unit or Component Testing

Definition

A test level that focuses on individual hardware or software components.

Reasonability

Software Engineer

Importance

Without the proper validation of each individual component with a software application or system, further test levels would fail as this is the foundation of key features developed.

System and/or Integration Testing

Definition

A test level that focuses on interactions between systems.

Reasonability

Software Engineer or Software Tester

Importance

Without the proper validation of the integration between components within an application or multiple applications, key data needed to deliver a higher-level business function can fail.

User Acceptance Testing

Definition

A test level was performed to determine if intended users accept the system.

Reasonability

Business or End-User

Importance

Without the proper validation of the user interface as intended to be designed, user function or satisfaction could be impacted negatively or cause unneeded additional manual work.

Post Production Testing

Definition

A test level performed after the release of the software product on the client site or in its intended or production environment or when the product has gone live.

Reasonability

Business or End-User

Importance

Without the proper validation of the application as intended to be designed in a real-world environment, user function or satisfaction could be impacted negatively or cause unneeded additional manual work. Even worse, it causes a loss of customers.

Chapter 2 – Basics: Planning

Strategy

In order to complete "software testing", a great deal of effort is needed upfront to help set the direction on how to prep and complete the testing activity. The core function of testing is to validate expected results. Having clear requirements for what the software needs to do is key. The initial requirements help software testers in many ways, such as prep and communication.

Prep

In regard to prepping for test execution many areas need to be addressed within your test strategy.

To simplify, we have added a list of 5 key items to research and understand.

Understand the Requirements

Requirements will either be fully defined or an incremental approach. Either way, to properly test you will need to have a full grasp on what is being delivered to the end user.

Understand the Design

Design is equally important to understand as some features might be enabled or disabled based on technology used or user preference.

Understand the Timeline for Delivery

As within any company, shareholders and executives are looking for the most efficient use of funds to complete strategic objectives. Many project timelines are time-based and leave all the testing activity crunched. Now that you know the requirements and the design, you can begin to get a gut check on how long these validations will take. Be sure to communicate to the stakeholders the amount of time you estimate needing to complete the proper validations.

Understand the Test Data

Most applications will require data to function. Some of these systems will be new, which makes getting the right test data a challenge. If you are testing an existing system, data for testing is more plentiful. Test data challenges have evolved over the years such the advancement of DevOps and Data Privacy. In this series, we will have a book just on test data.

Understand if any Constraints

In recent years, software development architecture is built on API's which are service level calls to request and receive data. In large companies, there are many development teams with different priorities. If one development team doesn't deliver an API on the same timeline as the overall application, you will face a constraint in validating those features.

Some newer techniques such as service virtualization have evolved to help mitigate risk of a defect or bug in production but is not a foolproof way to validate. Service virtualization is very technical and usually executed by the developer and not a traditional software tester.

Communication

As you learn more about what you need to validate, you will find out key risks that need to be communicated. A good portion of being a valuable software tester is having excellent communication. Knowing what to look for and who to communicate it too really helps drive the likelihood of launching a successful product or service. As you advance in your career, you will realize that proper terms matter. **You will want to voice any concerns or risk to the right audience, at the right time.**

For example, waiting to voice a concern about not completing requirements during development when launching the product into production is horrible timing for executives. This should have occurred during your planning phase when development likely just started.

Chapter 3 – Basics: Execution and Logging

The Fun Begins

Now that all the boring prep work is done, the fun begins! Most people that are software testers have a high level of curiosity and passion for breaking things! While it might seem like more fun to spend a majority of your time doing exploratory testing vs prep, prep does go a long way in improving your efficiency to validate and still meet the timeline demands you face.

As you begin executing test cases, this is the moment in time that truly lets you see the quality level of the application. When you execute tests, it's best practice to log the pass/fail results along with any **bug** or **defects** found. At most companies, they track this effort in a test management tool or system.

Definition

Bug or Defect - An imperfection or deficiency in a work product where it does not meet its requirements or specifications.

Reasonability

Software Engineer

Importance

The logging of a bug or defect is critical to improve the quality of a product or service. This logging notifies the creator or supporter of the software code and allows them the chance to fix the issue. The resolution from the software engineer is required before you can validate the test case.

Remember the goal of software testing is to identify issues in the quality of the product as part of quality check. Software testers do not introduce the actual bugs or defects unless they conduct a unit level test on their own code.

As a software tester typically validates after component development and testing, you must partner with the creator of the software to work with them on a resolution to fix. This partnership is an important bond to form as it can really make or break a new application and a successful launch.

As defects or bugs are fixed, the best practice is to re-test and validate the fix that occurred.

Some defects will cause a brief delay in executing your other downstream **test cases**. Understanding impacts to your other test cases and setting a priority of defects to be resolved is also what makes a great software tester.

Definition

Test Case - A set of preconditions, inputs, actions (where applicable), expected results and postconditions, developed based on test conditions.

Reasonability

Software Tester

Importance

Test cases are a critical part of software testing. Test cases hold the logical or process steps (preconditions) you have to take in order to execute the validation (postconditions). Test Cases are typically written in alignment with the requirements of the features in the software.

Automation

Automation setup is a key difference for companies as it reduces the need to manually setup test data and run test cases. It does not replace the need for a software tester. Software testers will always have a place in either setup of scripts or validating automation scripts and communicating risks, along with providing insight into the quality of the product. Automation cannot replace the visual testing that still needs to occur.

Later in this series of software testing books, we go over all things' automation such as history, frameworks, and what are best practices in regard to software testing.

Chapter 4 – Basics: Debugging, Re-testing, and Regression

Debugging

As a software tester a good portion of your time will be spent looking at possible defects or bugs and trying to determine if it's a true issue. As you log these issues, the developer assigned typically tries to re-create these in their environment. You will likely need to explain in detail the steps you took to produce the issue. This is usually a conversation directly with the creator of the software to determine if it's a true issue or maybe a test execution error.

As conversations and research moves forward between software tester and engineer, the software engineer spends time reviewing code, test data, and infrastructure as part of **debugging**.

Definition

Debugging - The process of finding, analyzing and removing the causes of failures in a component or system.

Reasonability

Software Engineer

Importance

Debugging is critical as it confirms or denies if an issue actually exists in the code, test data, or infrastructure. Once an issue is found, resolution can occur. If the issue is related to test data, the defect or bug is typically canceled as it's not a true issue in the code or infrastructure.

Re-testing (aka Confirmation Testing)

Once an issue is solidified as a defect or bug, the creator of the software will need to fix it. As this gets fixed, you as the software tester will need to re-execute your same test.

This might require you to spend some time resetting test data and re-logging test results. **Re-testing** or **confirmation testing** is simply re-executing the same test to help you validate the issue is now gone.

Definition

Re-testing or **Confirmation Testing** - A type of change-related testing performed after fixing a defect to confirm that a failure caused by that defect does not recur.

Reasonability

Software Tester

Importance

Re-testing or confirmation testing is important to give closure to an issue that was previously logged by the software tester and corrected by the software engineer. It's a mutual agreement between the creator of the software and the person validating the software features meet the requirement.

Regression

As software applications and systems evolve, more and more tests need to be executed to make sure old functionality has not been broken for enhancements. In regard to software testing, these tests are called **regression**. These are test cases that are typically run over and over again expecting the same results to ensure no other system issues occurred when introducing new functionality.

These tests validate existing features not impacted by current code changes. These types of tests are a great candidate to automate as they typically require the same test data and same results consistently. Please check out later series on automation to go overall all automation best practices.

Definition

Regression - A type of change-related testing to detect whether defects have been introduced or uncovered in unchanged areas of the software.

Reasonability

Software Tester

Importance

As software features are continuously added and integrated, some level of regression is needed. This validation makes sure no new bugs or defects are a result of new features being added. These tests are against old features that have already been tested in previous releases of the software.

Chapter 5 – Basics: Intro into Functional vs. Non-functional

Functional Testing

Functional testing is testing performed to evaluate if a component or system satisfies functional requirements. You can think of this as more of the visual or blocks of features that need to function. Most people think of testing as this type of testing only.

Non-Functional Testing

Non-functional testing is testing performed to evaluate whether a component or system complies with non-functional requirements. In other words, this is typically non-visual and can cover the validation of performance, security, or scaling of the application. In the series, we have a book just on non-functional testing.

White Box Testing

White box testing is a term used to validate the internal structure of a component of system when it's known. This validation is usually based on the software tester reviewing the actual code and design documents.

Black Box Testing

Black box testing is a term used to validate the internal structure of a component of system when it's <u>NOT</u> known. This validation is usually based on perception and logical steps the end-user of the software will take. The software tester cannot "see" what the innerworkings are.

Chapter 6 – Basics: Testing Tools

Spreadsheets

Many great software testers have started with just spreadsheets to track their test cases for pass/fail results. While this is a good start, it doesn't easily communicate well in larger companies and remote workers.

Test Management Tools

Many tools exist to help solve the communication problems that spreadsheets have. These tools hold uniformity and audit history that many large companies need. We are not going to give any recommendations at this time but as a software tester, it is advised to learn about these tools and if possible, take some certifications that can help set you apart if new to the software testing profession.

Software Development Backlog

Similar to software test management tools are software development backlog tools. These tools help project teams prioritize work for software engineers and testers. Any issues logged from testing usually feed into a test management system and a development backlog. Learn how to function in these backlogs as it will help you organize and track the progress of your testing activities and help software engineers know how testing is going.

Conclusion

Over time... software development and testing best practices evolve, keeping current with new technology and knowing how to test them is always a challenge.

The software testing community is expanding rapidly and becoming more specialized. This requires an open mind to see what is possible and challenge what's possible to assure software testing is keeping up with technology changes.

The mindset of being a software tester is consistent and strong over the decades, technology is not. Learn the basics and then expand. Have a solid background on key software testing concepts and communicating those best practices to key assuring stakeholders.

My hope is this series will help new and current software testers navigate the world of software testing. Not only advancing your knowledge in software testing, but also enable options into broader software quality management best practices or educate others.

The opportunities to enhance yourself are endless. You can focus on broad quality management which covers assurance and control or specialize in a particular area within quality control (i.e. software testing). Only you can determine which path you would like to take!

If you enjoyed this volume on software testing, please stay connected as we release future books on software testing.

Further Reference

The creation of this series is in partnership with Apply QA, LLC; a leading provider of best practices and consultation services for software quality assurance best practices.

Please visit https://www.applyqa.com to check out their products and services. In fact, the founder and CEO is Michael himself.

Other References

ISTQB Glossary https://glossary.istqb.org/en/search/

Merriam-Webster https://www.merriam-webster.com/dictionary/software